BREAKING THE ICE

T0348052

Kieran Lynn

BREAKING THE ICE

OBERON BOOKS
LONDON

WWW.OBERONBOOKS.COM

First published in 2016 by Oberon Books Ltd

521 Caledonian Road, London N7 9RH

Tel: +44 (0) 20 7607 3637 / Fax: +44 (0) 20 7607 3629

e-mail: info@oberonbooks.com

www.oberonbooks.com

Copyright © Kieran Lynn, 2016

Kieran Lynn is hereby identified as author of this play in accordance with section 77 of the Copyright, Designs and Patents Act 1988. The author has asserted his moral rights.

All rights whatsoever in this play are strictly reserved and application for performance etc. should be made before commencement of rehearsal to Berlin Associates, 7 Tyers Gate, London SE1 3HX. No performance may be given unless a licence has been obtained, and no alterations may be made in the title or the text of the play without the author's prior written consent.

You may not copy, store, distribute, transmit, reproduce or otherwise make available this publication (or any part of it) in any form, or binding or by any means (print, electronic, digital, optical, mechanical, photocopying, recording or otherwise), without the prior written permission of the publisher. Any person who does any unauthorized act in relation to this publication may be liable to criminal prosecution and civil claims for damages.

A catalogue record for this book is available from the British Library.

PB ISBN: 9781786820396

E ISBN: 9781786820402

Cover illustration by James Illman

Visit www.oberonbooks.com to read more about all our books and to buy them. You will also find features, author interviews and news of any author events, and you can sign up for e-newsletters so that you're always first to hear about our new releases.

Breaking the Ice received its world premiere in September 2016 at the Òran Mór, Glasgow as part of the A Play, A Pie and A Pint Autumn Season and was presented in association with the Traverse Theatre, Edinburgh.

Steven McNicoll
Jimmy Chisholm
Nicola Roy

Director, Tony Cownie
Designer, Kenneth MacLeod
Producers, April Chamberlain & Morag Fullarton
Assoc Producer, Sarah MacFarlane

With thanks to all the creative team at the Òran Mór.

Characters

This play is written for three actors – One actor plays Frank throughout, while the other two divide the remaining roles.

FRANK – Foreign and Commonwealth Office – Chief Scientific Advisor to the Arctic Council

IMO REP – UK International Maritime Organisation Representative

GIRL – Works at the Hotel Jack London

SHOP – A local shopkeeper

ACTIVIST 1 – The leader of a militant activist group called the Forest Owls

ACTIVIST 2 – A new recruit to the Forest Owls

CALL CENTRE WORKER – An underpaid call centre worker

SECURITY GUARD – The car park attendant at the FCO

ANSWERING MACHINE – Automated voice recording

COP – A local Police Officer

OIL EXECUTIVE – A Senior Executive at North Atlantic Energy

PROFESSOR – Public Policy to the Canadian Minister for Foreign Affairs and an adjunct Professor of Ethics at the University of Eastern Manitoba

ANNOUNCER – The Chair of the Arctic Council

US MARINE – In charge of security at the stage door

FRANK MONTGOMERY, FCO Chief Scientific Advisor to the Arctic Council, is centre stage. He wears a white, bathrobe, with the initials H. J. L. stitched on the lapel. He addresses the audience.

FRANK: Well, I suppose I'll start at the very beginning. I arrived in Barrow, Alaska yesterday evening. It was all a little last minute. I had only been in the post of FCO Chief Scientific Advisor to the Arctic Council for one week – After the previous advisor was struck down with a crippling case of ultraviolet keratitis, more commonly known as snow-blindness. I was hurriedly suggested and appointed based on my work as a geologist – I was then given two days to write a speech to present at the Arctic Council meeting. The Arctic Council, in case you don't know, is the intergovernmental forum composed of the eight nations that border the Arctic – Norway, Sweden, Finland, Denmark, Iceland, Russia, Canada, and the United States. I was to be giving a speech called, The Proposed Impacts of Progressive Economic Expansion in the Arctic. Needless to say, I hadn't expected a large turnout. Anyway, I had taken my speech on the plane, to practise during the flight, and I accidently left it on-board. I put it in the pocket in the seat in front of me during the serving of the meal and had forgotten to take it out after the plane landed. I called the airline, Air Greenland, but by the time I called them the plane was half way to Nuuk. So I stayed up all night writing a new speech, or rather trying to remember the old speech. Then this morning, while putting finishing touches on it

during breakfast, I accidentally spilled yogurt on
my suit. I knew selecting yogurt from the buffet it
was a mistake. I'm a geologist, which means I rarely
get invited anywhere, formally or informally, and
I was feeling excited. Anyway, the foil lid of the
yogurt was a real tricky one, so I adjusted my arm
to give it a little more muscle. I ripped the thing
off with too much force and the yogurt splattered
all over my lap. I'm digressing here, I know I am,
it's simply because I'm still frustrated at myself.
Yogurt? What was I thinking? Fortunately for me, the
hotel had a dry cleaning service. So I changed into
my dressing gown and sent my suit to be cleaned.
During this time, the UK representative at the IMO
came to see me – That's the International Maritime
Organisation – In fact, I should say at this point, that
the acronyms at work in international relations are
simply staggering. A few days ago I found myself in a
meeting with the MD of the PRD for the FCO of the
UK. I didn't know if we were going to talk about the
Arctic or play Scrabble. And the afternoon after my
speech I've been invited to a WIP with a lady from
the BDSM – Turns out that's the British Directorate
of Strategy in Mining, so I'm hoping we won't need
to agree on a safe word. Anyway, I was visited by a
chap from the IMO who wanted to talk me through
shipping lanes.

Cut to:

A large map of the Arctic appears. IMO REP, the UK representative at the International Maritime Organisation, is presenting in front of it. FRANK is trying to pay attention to the presentation and write his speech at the same time.

IMO REP: Right, let's go over it once more.

FRANK: We've just been over it. And I really should work on my speech.

IMO REP: I know, but this is important to us and there will be a section for questions at the end so you have to sound like you know what you're talking about.

FRANK: I can assure you it's going to take a lot longer than this to make it sound like I know what I'm talking about.

IMO REP uses the map to talk FRANK through it.

IMO REP: The Northeast Passage runs from northern Norway east along the north Russian coast. It traverses the Barents Sea, the Kara Sea, the Laptev Sea, the East Siberian Sea and the Chukchi Sea, through the Bering Strait and then the west coast of the United States, or the coast of East Asia is your oyster. China, Japan, South Korea, in three quarters of the time it would have taken to travel south through the Suez. And this way we don't have to run the risk of Somalia pirates or the Strait of Malacca.

FRANK: Will there ever be Arctic pirates?

IMO REP: Maybe eventually, but it's cold up there so we'll have to give them time to invest in winter wardrobes.

FRANK: Arctic pirates.

IMO REP: Yes.

FRANK: I'm sure they'll be deadly and murderous and so on, but you've got to admit Arctic Pirates gets the imagination going, doesn't it?

IMO REP: I suppose it does.

FRANK: I imagine them in reindeer fur coats and holding bows and arrows.

IMO REP: Well, they'll probably be wearing North Face jackets and holding Russian-made Kalashnikovs, but I'm glad you're enjoying a flight of fancy. *(He goes back to the charts.)* The Northwest Passage is traversable, but is complicated by thick ice, complex straights and pingos that make navigation tricky...

FRANK: Pingo.

IMO REP: And require...

FRANK: Pingo.

IMO REP: Advanced ice breaking.

FRANK: Pingo.

IMO REP: Yes pingo. I said pingo. What about it?

FRANK: Pingo.

IMO REP: Yes, it's a, you know what we've been through this twice, it's an earth covered ice cap. A small mound. Looks like earth, but has ice underneath.

FRANK: I know what it is. It's just such an unusual word. Pingo.

IMO REP: It's an Inuvialukton word. It means small hill.

FRANK: I'm not sure I'll be able to say it without smiling.

IMO REP: You can use the scientific term if you prefer.

FRANK: What is that again?

IMO REP: Hydrolaccolith.

FRANK: ...Pingo is easier to remember.

IMO REP: Exactly. The Northwest Passage is also subject to disputes. The Canadians claim that it is not an international strait, but rather an extension of their internal waters, which could make far more bureaucratic and expensive to cross. However, we expect as the Arctic sea ice continues to reduce, shipping lanes will continue to open up and global pressure will force the Canadians to retract their claims. But for now it is still a little too risky so we're mostly staying out of it. Any questions so far?

FRANK: Is it cold here?

IMO REP: In Alaska? No, it isn't. The polar bears just live here because they like American food.

FRANK: I don't mean Alaska, I mean in this room. I'm feeling a little cold.

IMO REP: That is probably just your dressing gown. I hear they can be a little draughty.

FRANK: My room is very warm. Of course, it is in the basement next to some kind of boiler that creaked and kept me awake all night, but hard to argue with the temperature.

IMO REP: You should be grateful that you have a room. When I first started in the Foreign and Commonwealth Office I was sent to assist the Ambassador to Morocco at the African Economic Community forum in Mozambique. I slept in a caravan in the hotel car park and was cooked to a crisp every single night. By the time I went home, I'd lost half a stone.

FRANK: Why did FCO go to the African Economic Community forum?

IMO REP: We're Britain, Frank, we go everywhere. Diplomatically speaking there isn't a country that we either haven't been in bed with, don't want to get in bed with or isn't desperate to get into bed with us. It makes selling Manchester United shirts easy, but puts a lot of miles on the diplomats.

FRANK: Diplomat. I can't believe you're talking about me when you say that. Oh, actually that reminds me. Look at this.

FRANK picks a box of business cards off the table and shows IMO REP one.

FRANK: They had new business cards made for the Council meeting. Frank Montgomery. Chief Scientific Advisor.

IMO REP: That's wonderful.

FRANK: Of course the real beauty is not what it says, but rather in the way it says it. Rub your thumb across it.

IMO REP: Excuse me?

FRANK: Go ahead.

IMO REP: You want me to rub my thumb across your business card?

FRANK: Yes.

IMO REP: I've had some offers in my time, but this is honestly new ground.

FRANK: It's the most breathtaking embossing that I think I've ever known. Feel it.

IMO REP: I don't want to feel it.

FRANK: Very professional, spared no expense. Feel it.

IMO REP: I don't want to feel your business card.

FRANK: Give me your thumb.

IMO REP: No.

FRANK: Yes.

IMO REP: No!

FRANK: Give me your thumb!

FRANK grabs IMO REP's thumb and runs it over his business card.

IMO REP: …Oh I say.

FRANK: I know!

IMO REP: That really is something. It kind of makes me wish I was blind.

FRANK: Of course, I don't know where the phone number actually links to, since I don't keep a desk at the Foreign and Commonwealth Office, but with embossing like this who cares.

IMO REP: We should get on with the briefing? We're getting a little tight on time.

FRANK: Yes, I'm sorry, like I said I'm very excited. This is my first one of these and I'm still not sure what will happen.

IMO REP: I'll tell you what's going to happen Frank, and the reason I know this is because it happens at every meeting, not just of the Arctic Council, but at almost every meeting that Russia and the United States attend. We spend several days listening to all of the vested parties. We hear from member states, we hear from observer states, we hear from indigenous communities and we hear from NGO's. It's a week of spirited debate and provocative discussion, at the conclusion of which everybody flies homes and Russia and the United States do whatever they want anyway regardless of what was discussed.

FRANK: And what do we want to get out of it?

IMO REP: Honestly? We don't care what happens, we just what a piece of it when it does. Are oil companies going to drill in the Arctic? Yes. Will shipping routes open up? Yes. Will military installations be built? Yes. We're not going to push anything through and we're not going to stand in anything's way. And if anything does go down we'll want a cut of it. And do you want to know why?

FRANK: Because we're British.

IMO REP: You might have a career in diplomacy after all. Now, I'd like to talk to you a little about the Russian Continental Shelf. Basically, this is a shelf of rock beneath the Arctic Ocean north of Russia. If Russia can prove that this shelf is an extension of their territory then we're all in big trouble.

FRANK: There's a severe shortage of pastries in this breakfast.

IMO REP: I'm going to go out on a limb and say that I don't have your full attention.

FRANK: Aren't Denmark one of the principle contributors to this forum?

IMO REP: Yes.

FRANK: And aren't pastries one of Denmark's signature exports?

IMO REP: Yes, just behind Lego and Hamlet.

FRANK: I'll bring it up with them. The first Dane I meet I'll say, I was surprised, no perturbed, by the lack of your country's signature viennoiserie.

IMO REP: …I think you should.

FRANK: Do you?

IMO REP: Yes, in fact, I think we should add it to the agenda.

FRANK: Oh, you're making fun of me.

IMO REP: I'll see if we can find some time between the updating of the Arctic Search and Rescue Agreement and the discussion on the categorisation of species for the Conservation of Arctic Flora and Fauna. In fact, maybe we should bump that from the schedule completely and replace with a new topic entitled, "The lack of Danish pastries in the Hotel Jack London."

FRANK: Well, I'm not sure we need to go that far.

IMO REP: You have to focus Frank. These events run on status. If other countries feel like you don't know what you're talking about then it starts to lower our position of power.

FRANK: Don't worry. I have an MSc and a Ph.D. from Cambridge, I've won the Benedict Medal, I've won the Ridgewell Medal and I've been on the Prime Minister's advisory council for energy for the last five years.

IMO REP: That may be true Frank, but you have also just spilled a full apricot yogurt on your suit and the speech you're about to give is currently on an aeroplane in Greenland, so I'm just covering my bases.

GIRL enters – She works at the hotel and could clear plates or top up coffees.

GIRL: Your suit is almost ready. How was everything with your breakfast?

IMO REP: Don't get him started.

FRANK: Everything is fine, although I do have one request.

GIRL: Yes.

FRANK: Tea.

GIRL: Tea?

FRANK: Tea. It seems this hotel only serves coffee.

GIRL: We have herbal tea.

FRANK: Yes, but I'm afraid that is not tea.

GIRL: It has tea in the name?

FRANK: Well, it's a type of tea, but I'm afraid it's not the type I'm looking for. I'm looking for English tea, builders' tea, Earl Grey. Any of those present?

GIRL: I'll go and check.

The GIRL exits.

IMO REP: Your speech is at 12:30 until 1:00pm, and we're breaking at one o'clock approximately for lunch. You'd better finish promptly, or they will cut you off. These people take their lunch breaks very seriously. Especially the Russians. The American's don't mind, they see the taking of breaks as a sign of weakness and usually stay at their tables drinking coffee and eating cold sandwiches. Got it? One o'clock. Finish.

FRANK: Yes. I will do my best.

The GIRL enters.

FRANK: Ah, and here is the girl with the tea.

GIRL: Actually, we don't have any, I'm afraid.

FRANK: I can't remember the last time I didn't start my day with a cup of tea.

GIRL: You should try the store next door.

FRANK: I would, but I don't have a lot of time and my suit is being cleaned.

GIRL: It's only next door, you can just go there in your robe?

FRANK: Really?

GIRL: Absolutely. People do it all the time. They're usually going for alcohol in the middle of the night, but they do it all the same.

FRANK: Seems a little strange.

GIRL: Trust me. It's right next door.

The GIRL exits. FRANK addresses the audience.

FRANK: Perhaps it was the intoxication of the Arctic air, or the lingering thrill that only good embossing can provide, but I decided to do something out of character and venture out into the wide world in search of tea. I soon discovered, however, that next door in Barrow is not like next door in Edinburgh, and before I knew it I was tramping a few hundred metres hoping desperately no one would see me. Anyway, eventually I made it to the store and was greeted by a man who made polar bears look inviting.

Cut to:

A convenience store. A rough and ready place with a pioneer feel. A SHOPKEEPER enters.

FRANK: Excuse me sir.

SHOP: You bastards are getting earlier and earlier every year. The beers are in the fridge and I keep the hard stuff behind the counter. I also sell weed and prescription medication.

FRANK: No, I'm not... Prescription... No, I don't want any of that. I'm looking for tea.

SHOP: T? Is that a street name?

FRANK: No, it is the actual name.

SHOP: What is it?

FRANK: What is tea? It's tea. You put it in a cup and drink it.

SHOP: Like ice tea? Yeh, we sell that. It's next to the meat fridge.

FRANK: No, not ice tea. Tea. Hot tea.

SHOP: Herbal tea? Yeh, it's next to the meat fridge too.

FRANK: No, not herbal tea. English breakfast.

SHOP: We sell breakfast in a can. It's near...

FRANK: Near the meat fridge? Yes, seems that's where I could find most things. But actually, not *an* English Breakfast, but rather English Breakfast the variety of tea. Or Earl Grey, Lady Grey or any other variety?

SHOP: I don't think we've got it. But you should check near the meat fridge.

FRANK: Why not? Seems that's where everything else is.

FRANK begins exploring the store.

SHOP: You're here for the conference?

FRANK: The Arctic Council, yes, that's correct.

SHOP: What do you do there?

FRANK: I don't really know actually, this will be my first conference.

SHOP: No, I mean what do *you* do there?

FRANK: Oh, I'm the Foreign and Commonwealth Office Chief Scientific Advisor. Would you like to see a business card, it's wonderfully embossed?

SHOP: Can I give you a piece of advice?

FRANK: Is it about finding tea?

SHOP: Don't listen to the greens.

FRANK: Excuse me?

SHOP: The environmentalists. Don't listen to them. They don't know what they're talking about.

FRANK: Okay.

SHOP: None of them live here. None of them even visit here. They sit at home in huge houses, full of electronics and clothes and furniture and then tell the people who live up here not to build stuff in case we upset the lynx, or the polar bears, or the icebergs. They'll see us starve, poor and out on the streets before they'll take an acre off a polar bear or build a road through a forest.

FRANK: Yes, well I'm sure they're legitimate concerns.

SHOP: We need jobs here. We need money. Young people need something that they can work towards. Otherwise they just leave for the cities.

FRANK: I don't mean to be rude sir, but I am wearing a bathrobe and I really just came here for tea.

SHOP: Of course you did. You fly in and out, without spending any time in these places. If you did you'd see what life is like up here. Infant mortality is high, substance abuse is high, and the only thing that is going to pull us out of that is a strong economy. Money for schools, doctors, and community centres. Now, I like the arctic fox as much as the next guy, but he isn't going to put food on the table and he won't cure you if you get sick. You get what I'm saying?

FRANK: I'm getting most of what you're saying, although you lost me around the time an arctic fox was putting food on the table.

SHOP: Trust me, we need development here. I'm sorry we didn't have the tea you were looking for, but if you need any weed later you come and see me.

FRANK: Yes sir. Thank you, I'll keep that in mind.

SHOP exits.

FRANK: I had ventured in search of glory and I had failed. Time was getting short, so in defeat I began to trudge back towards the hotel, but barely made it half way before…

We hear the sound of an engine revving, the screeching of brakes, and a van door opening.

Two people wearing children's wolf masks appear. They grab FRANK, put a bag over his head, and drag him into darkness.

We hear the van doors slam and the van drives away.

Cut to:

We're in the van as it drives around the streets. FRANK is in the middle surrounded by two members of militant activist group THE FOREST OWLS. 1 is a veteran, 2 is a rookie.

FRANK: Now, just what the heck is going here? If this is about the shopkeeper, I didn't buy anything off him, I wouldn't even know how to take weed.

1: You're Frank Montgomery. Is that correct?

FRANK: Yes, it is.

1: Frank Montgomery, the scientific advisor?

FRANK: You know, I think prisoners of war are only supposed to reveal their name, rank and serial number. Although I don't have a rank. Or a serial number, I suppose. And this isn't really war, is it?

1: Shut up!

FRANK: Okay. Sorry. I ramble when I'm nervous. Plus, I'm only wearing this dressing gown and nudity, even partial, has always made me uncomfortable.

2: You're here to make a recommendation to the Council?

FRANK: How did you know that?

2: It's on the agenda.

2 takes out a copy of the agenda.

FRANK: Oh, how fun. I haven't seen this yet. Oh, no, they spelled my second name wrong.

2: What will be the nature of your recommendation?

FRANK: Excuse me?

1: What are you going to tell them?

FRANK: You want to hear my speech?

2: You're going to tell them that shipping routes should be exploited?

FRANK: I really don't think I should tell you very much, this is highly unusual, and I'm just not sure of my footing here.

2 slaps FRANK's face.

FRANK: Ow!

1: What are you doing?

2: I'm sorry. I got carried away.

1: I told you not to hit him. I was absolutely clear about that.

2: I'm sorry. I don't know why I did it. This is my first kidnapping.

1: What? You said you'd done it before. In Brazil?

2: No, I was just an intern then. I was in charge of the logistics, but I wasn't actually on the kidnapping.

1: Logistics? What logistics?

2: Well I rented the van, I arranged the hideout, and I placed the anonymous call to police.

1: When you explained your role to me you made it seem like you played a far more active role than that.

2: Can I be honest?

1: Yes.

2: I was afraid that if you didn't think I had enough experience that you wouldn't let me come with you.

1: Well, that would certainly have crossed my mind.

2: But I want to be part of the kidnapping team. I didn't become a militant activist so I could spend my days booking hire vans and mopping up blood.

FRANK: Did you say blood?

1: I probably would have still picked you, but now I'm feeling conflicted.

2: Because I've been dishonest?

1: Because you've been dishonest. Exactly. How will I know that I can ever trust anything you say again?

2: Please, you can. Everything else was true, I just exaggerated a little so that I could be a part of the kidnap squad.

1: Well, we're here now. And you were doing a very good job up until that slap.

2: I'm sorry, I don't know where that came from.

1: Just try to keep it under control. It's easy to go overboard in these situations, but actually it is restraint that is a far more effective threat.

2: That's so true. Thank you for the advice.

1: That's what I'm here for.

FRANK: I hate to interrupt this, but I'm due to give a speech soon. Now I don't want to risk another slap in the face, but I was just wondering was there a reason you brought me here?

Silence.

2: Do you know anything about walrus?

FRANK: Walrus?

2: Walrus.

FRANK: I'm afraid I don't.

1: An increase of traffic through the Bering Strait will affect the migratory routes of bowhead whales and walrus. You're going to recommend that the Northeast Passage remains closed to prevent impacting the wildlife.

FRANK: Impacting the walrus?

2: Fishing rights, drilling rights, whaling rights, mining rights, transport rights, military rights. We can't let the Arctic Ocean turn into the English Channel.

FRANK: Is there whaling in the English Channel?

1: You know what we mean.

FRANK: I do know what you mean. And we will do all that we can to ensure that any expansion into Arctic waters is properly considered and responsible.

2: …Said like a true diplomat.

FRANK: Was it? Thank you. You know, this is my first week and I'm not sure I've mastered the tone.

2: The Arctic is melting as a result of human activity. It is unbelievable that, instead of trying to prevent further melting, companies are queuing up to explore new forms of exploitation.

1: Right now, oil and gas companies are looking at maps of the Arctic and making plans to drill, shipping companies are looking at new routes and militaries are devising strategies to control it all.

FRANK: Yes, I suspect they probably are, but I'm really not sure what you want me to do about it. I'm just an advisor. I can make recommendations, but since when do governments listen to scientists?

1: Your opinion will be heard.

FRANK: It might be heard, but I doubt it will be listened to.

2: It will be more than the animals that live here.

FRANK: Well that is true, but it is hardly my fault that polar bears can't speak.

1: When the Council meets we want you to recommend that shipping lanes remain closed.

FRANK: Again, I'm not sure that I can do that.

1: You can, and you will.

2: Otherwise, you're going to get worse than a slap in the face.

1: A lot worse.

2: A thousand times worse.

1: A million times worse.

2: We'll chop you up into little pieces and feed you to our dogs.

1: Again, you've just taken it a little too far.

2: Sorry.

1: Don't worry about it. You'll learn. Let's get him out of here.

The van screeches to a halt and FRANK is thrown to the ground.

FRANK: Ow.

Cut to:

We're on the side of the road, in the middle of nowhere. FRANK stands and looks around.

FRANK: They threw me on the ground and drove away. I didn't see their registration and I never saw their faces. I had no idea where I was, or how I would get back into town. The only civilized thing that I could see was a public phone across the road. I ran towards it, though the only phone number I knew off by heart was my own, and I suspected quite correctly, that calling myself would be less than useful since I wouldn't be home to help me. Anyway, I reached into my pocket and momentarily believed I had found salvation.

He takes out the business card from earlier.

FRANK: My business card. Yes! My god, that is good embossing.

FRANK dials the number on the business card.

A phone is ringing. It is picked up, by a CALL CENTRE WORKER.

CALL CENTRE: FCO, how can I assist you?

FRANK: Hello this is Frank Montgomery, I'm Chief Scientific Advisor to the Arctic Council.

CALL CENTRE: And how can I help?

FRANK: Well, I don't know really. I've been taken.

CALL CENTRE: Taken where?

FRANK: I don't know.

CALL CENTRE: And how can I assist you?

FRANK: I need help. I've been taken.

CALL CENTRE: What have you been taking?

FRANK: No, I *was* taken. By some activists. They were wearing masks and they demanded that I block all shipping permit applications in the Bering Strait.

CALL CENTRE: Are you calling about a permit application?

FRANK: No. Listen, carefully, I'm going to explain this as simply as I can. I'm Frank Montgomery. I'm the Chief Scientific Advisor to the Arctic Council.

CALL CENTRE: Okay.

FRANK: I've been… I'm a little reluctant to use this word. But I believe I have just been kidnapped.

CALL CENTRE: …Who has been kidnapped?

FRANK: I think that I have.

CALL CENTRE: You think?

FRANK: I know. I have been kidnapped.

CALL CENTRE: Now?

FRANK: No, not now.

CALL CENTRE: When?

FRANK: A few minutes ago.

CALL CENTRE: And are you still being held?

FRANK: No, they've just released me.

CALL CENTRE: Then what do you need us for?

FRANK: Because they've stranded me in the middle of nowhere, with no way of getting back to my hotel and I've got about half an hour before I have to give a seminal speech which I haven't finished writing yet. So can you please help me figure out a way of getting in touch with someone who can help me?

CALL CENTRE: Well, you've actually come through to the Office of External Enquires, it sounds like you need the Office of Internal Security. Hold on, I'll transfer you.

FRANK: No wait…

Too late, the call is transferred. An elderly SECURITY GUARD.

SECURITY GUARD: Security.

FRANK: Hello, I'm calling from Barrow.

SECURITY GUARD: In-Furness? That's nice. My wife is from Morecambe.

FRANK: Not Barrow-in-Furness.

SECURITY GUARD: No, Morecambe. Morecambe Bay, it's just around the corner.

FRANK: No, Alaska.

SECURITY GUARD: You'll ask her what?

FRANK: No. Not I'll ask her, Alaska. I'm in Alaska.

SECURITY GUARD: Well, what are you doing up there?

FRANK: I'm with the Foreign and Commonwealth Office. I'm calling because I've been taken.

SECURITY GUARD: Taken where?

FRANK: I don't know.

SECURITY GUARD: Well, I'm sorry but I can't help you find yourself, I'm at work.

FRANK: I need to report it. It could be a diplomatic incident. I've been kidnapped.

SECURITY GUARD: Kidnapped?

FRANK: Yes. Isn't this the Office of Internal Security?

SECURITY GUARD: No.

FRANK: No?

SECURITY GUARD: No, this is Building Security. I'm in charge of the car park.

FRANK: Well, can you transfer me to the Office of Internal Security?

SECURITY GUARD: I'll try, but I'm not very good with the phone.

The SECURITY GUARD begins bashing the keys and cursing under his breath about the stupid bloody phone.

SECURITY GUARD: Did that work?

FRANK: No, I'm still here.

SECURITY GUARD: Righto, I'll try again.

The SECURITY GUARD dials the phone again.

SECURITY GUARD: There we go.

We hear him put the phone down, but the line hasn't transferred.

FRANK: I'm still here.

But the SECURITY GUARD has gone about his business.

SECURITY GUARD: *(Singing.)* Working nine to five, what a way to make a living

FRANK: Hello? I'm still here, haven't transferred.

SECURITY GUARD: *(Humming.)* Hmm, hmm, hmm hmm hmm, it's all taking and no giving.

FRANK: Excuse me sir? I'm still on the phone.

SECURITY GUARD: It's enough do doo doo…

FRANK: I'm still here, you stupid old…

SECURITY GUARD: Hello.

FRANK: *(Immediately polite.)* Hello there, I just wanted to make you aware that you haven't actually transferred me yet. You need to press zero and then dial the number you want to transfer.

SECURITY GUARD: Alright, I'll give it another go.

FRANK: Yes, you do that you daft…

SECURITY GUARD: Did you say something?

FRANK: No, thank you very much for your help.

The ringing tone starts again. Until it is answered by an ANSWERING MACHINE – Efficient, friendly and emotionless.

ANSWERING MACHINE: Hello, you've reached the Department of Internal Security.

FRANK: Thank goodness, I need your help.

ANSWERING MACHINE: We are currently closed. Our opening hours are nine until five...

FRANK loses it. He screams at the pay phone and has a mini-fit. Shouting and hollering.

A Police siren sounds.

FRANK: And that was when you found me.

A COP enters.

Cut to:

An overnight jail cell. FRANK has been telling his story to the COP.

FRANK: So you see Officer, it was not a case of public intoxication and nudity, but rather a case of my being kidnapped while searching for tea. Now, I'm aware it's not an excuse you'll hear every day, but I'm hoping the level of excruciating detail, combined with my impeccable past record, will endear me to you.

COP: It makes sense. At least most of it, but you're going to have to give a full statement on the people who picked you up.

FRANK: I'd be more than happy too.

COP: The town swells up around these conferences, it's hard to keep track of who is coming and who is going.

FRANK: I can imagine.

COP: So you're a science guy?

FRANK: I suppose I am, yes.

COP: So you'll be mostly thinking about rocks and the weather and that kind of thing?

FRANK: …Something like that.

COP: Ever heard of Sami?

FRANK: Davis Junior? Yes, I've heard a lot about him, but I don't get a lot of time for the classics.

COP: Not, *that* Sammy. The Sami. I'm Sami.

FRANK: Well it's nice to meet you Sami.

COP: No, that's not my name. It's my… Sami are a
   people. They're my people. They live above the
   Arctic Circle.

FRANK: No, haven't heard of them.

COP: We're herders. Reindeer herders.

FRANK: That's sounds fascinating.

COP: It is. Do you know much about reindeer?

FRANK: Honestly, I can't say that I do. And I don't know
   anything about walrus, if that's your next question.

COP: The Sami live on a territory called Sápmi, which is
   incredibly rich in precious metals, oil and natural gas.

FRANK: Right.

COP: Now a few thousand of these Sami people still
   wish to live according to their customs and to herd
   their reindeer on the lands that they have always
   been free to roam. Only now, with ice melting,
   the oil companies are moving in, and the logging
   companies, and the mining companies it's becoming
   harder to do that. Roads are being built, dams are
   being built, wind farms, military bases, ports, and the
   Sami are getting pushed further and further out of the
   picture.

FRANK: Well, I'm sure that must be causing some conflict. And I really would love to talk more about it.

COP: Some? The Sami have been at constant conflict for a hundred years. Who do you think wins the fight, the electricity companies, the mining companies, the military, the shipping companies, and everyone else, or three thousand Eskimos who want to herd reindeer?

FRANK: I suppose you're right, but you know there isn't a lot that I can do about that.

COP: Yes, I hear that a lot.

FRANK: If there was anything I would, but it's not really my purpose here.

COP: What is your purpose here? Give the all-clear to the oil companies? Two thumbs up to the American, Russia and European mining companies, tell them they can do what they want as long as they dump all their toxic waste where no one will find it? What about the people who lived there before those countries even existed? The Aleut, the Inuit, the Sami, the Gwich'in. They don't get a look in.

FRANK: They are Permanent Participants in the meeting, they can attend whenever they like.

COP: At their own cost, but I'm guessing that the United States State Department has a considerably bigger budget for travel than the Inuit Circumpolar Council. Not to mention more lawyers, more muscle and the world's largest military standing behind it. Something tells me that the footing may not be quite equal between all parties. Anyway, maybe you're right, and it isn't your fault. But keep it in mind will you? There are people who live here. They shouldn't get bullied out.

FRANK: No, they shouldn't.

COP: I'm sorry I brought you down here, it's not everyday I see a man on a street attacking a payphone in a bathrobe.

FRANK: I can imagine. Can I ask you something?

COP: Of course.

FRANK: If you're Sami, and your people are reindeer herders then why are you here?

COP: I'm here for the same reason most people are where they are. I need the money. Come on, I'll give you a ride back to your hotel.

FRANK: I'll have to go directly to the conference centre actually, I'm due to speak soon.

An EXECUTIVE from an international energy company enters.

EXECUTIVE: Actually, if you don't mind Officer, I'll escort Dr. Montgomery. I'm heading that way anyway.

COP: Be my guest.

COP exits.

EXECUTIVE: Dr. Montgomery, I work for North Atlantic Energy.

FRANK: How do you do?

EXECUTIVE: Very well. My car is waiting outside.

Cut to:

FRANK and EXECUTIVE sit in the back seat of a luxury car.

FRANK: This is a nice car.

EXECUTIVE: Do you like nice things?

FRANK: That's a strange question.

EXECUTIVE: We're all very excited to hear you speak today.

FRANK: Oh, yes. Me too. I wonder what I'm going to say.

EXECUTIVE: So do we. You know, not to put too fine a point on it, but the science is entirely in our favour.

FRANK: Is it now?

EXECUTIVE: Yes, as are the economics, the world's governments, and the global economy.

FRANK: Right.

EXECUTIVE: But, as you know, these things are a constant exercise in public relations. And that is where we could always use help.

FRANK: Help?

EXECUTIVE: Can I tell you two of the most important words in the media?

FRANK: Are they "new subscriber"?

EXECUTIVE: No.

FRANK: "Advertising revenue'?

EXECUTIVE: No.

FRANK: "Page three"?

EXECUTIVE: They're "Scientists say".

FRANK: …

EXECUTIVE: Scientists say, "Sugar is good for you."
Scientists say, "Fruit makes your hair fall out."
Scientists say, "Masturbation makes you go blind."

FRANK: It doesn't, does it?

EXECUTIVE: There will be drilling in the Arctic. It's
inevitable. So, then the real question becomes, which
country will run the table?

FRANK: I'm not sure that is the real question.

EXECUTIVE: The United Kingdom has no claim of any
part of the Arctic. We're strictly an observer in the
Arctic Council and we will never have any territorial
claim. But, we have Shell, and we have BP, BHP
Billiton, Anglo American, Glencore, Rio Tinto and
BAE. We can still lead on this, but, and this is where
you come in, we need "Scientists say…".

FRANK: …

EXECUTIVE: In exchange we could fund your research,
your professorships, and, of course, we'll see that
you're well compensated.

FRANK: I don't know what to say.

EXECUTIVE: You don't have to say anything, at least not now. I'm going to give you my business card. You're going to go through the Council meeting, as usual. And if at some point in the future you feel like you want to talk to me, you can call and we'll talk. That's it.

EXECUTIVE hands FRANK a business card.

FRANK: Wow. This is really nice embossing.

EXECUTIVE: We're here.

FRANK: Oh, so we are.

EXECUTIVE: Just in time.

FRANK: Yes.

EXECUTIVE: I'm glad we found time to talk.

FRANK: ...Yes. Thank you for the lift.

EXECUTIVE: I'm looking forward to your speech.

FRANK: Thank you. I'm afraid I'm not.

FRANK steps out of the car.

The car drives away.

Cut to:

FRANK enters the Conference Centre. He approaches a PROFESSOR.

FRANK: Excuse me, can you point me in the direction of the Council meeting?

PROF: Of course, I'm actually heading that way myself. I'll walk with you.

FRANK: Oh, thank you that is kind.

PROF: It's on the second floor. The lift will be quicker.

PROF pushes button. They enter the lift.

PROF: I thought you might be looking for the steam room.

FRANK: Excuse me... Oh, the robe, yes, you'll have to excuse that, I've had a rather unusual day.

PROF: I don't mind. Anything to liven this place up.

FRANK: You're a diplomat?

PROF: Yes, that's right. I'm an advisor in Public Policy to the Canadian Minister for Foreign Affairs.

FRANK: Right.

PROF: I don't quite know how I ended up here. A doctorate in philosophy and I end up playing PR for the government.

FRANK: Well, speaking as a man in a convention centre lift in a dressing gown, life doesn't always go the way we planned.

The lift door opens. They walk to the right.

PROF: That's certainly true. It's this way.

FRANK: Philosophy, you said?

PROF: Yes, ethics.

FRANK: Interesting. I've been thinking a lot about ethics this morning. I'm not sure where I stand.

PROF: Right now you're on the second floor of the William McKinley Conference Centre.

FRANK: I meant ethically.

PROF: I know what you meant, there aren't many jokes you can make with ethics, I'm afraid we occasionally have to take the low hanging fruit.

FRANK: I know all about that, I'm a geologist. Why did the geologist take his girlfriend to a quarry?

PROF: I don't know.

FRANK: He wanted to get a little boulder.

PROF: Nice.

FRANK: Beggars can't be choosers. What do you make of the ethics of all of this?

They turn left.

PROF: Complicated. You see, our ethical principles traditionally only extend to the living. We feel a certain duty of care to other living things. Whether that is innate within us, or the result of our upbringing and moral tradition is not clear, and perhaps not important. It's this way.

They turn right.

PROF: We see a sick animal our yearning is to help that animal. We see a crying child or an injured old person, our yearning is to help that person. That would seem to be based on a morality that is universal and not reserved for humans.

The PROFESSOR is lost.

PROF: I think it's down here. An animal finding another animal in distress, for example, may kill that animal for his own sustenance, though it is just as common to observe compassion in animals, and contrary to what you might thing in cases where an animal does not understand it often leans towards compassion and not violence or destruction. This way.

They turn left.

PROF: The question is in what capacity does our morality extend to the non-living, more specifically, to places, in this case the Arctic? Just as we might believe that we have a moral obligation to protect and defend other living creatures, do we have the same moral obligation to protect places? Mountain ranges, a desert, or in this case a frozen continent.

FRANK stops.

FRANK: I think we've gone in a circle.

PROF: Have we?

FRANK: Yes, there is the lift.

PROF: Right, now I definitely know the way, it's down here.

They turn right.

FRANK: We'd better hurry.

They begin jogging.

PROF: We often find that our duty to protect a place is presented to us so as to appeal to our desire to help the living. We are told to save the rainforest to protect the creatures that live in it, we are told not to pollute the oceans for the sake of whales, fish, and the creatures that live there, we are asked to protect the Arctic for the sake of those that call it home.

Certainly there are few who would argue with that, but I'm beginning to wonder whether we have an innate right to protect and preserve places for their own merit. I think it's just down here.

FRANK: I've heard that before.

They turn left.

PROF: Of course, as it often is, questions of morality become one of a balance of scales. Certainly, any mineral exploitation, reduction in shipping cost and so on, would do more to raise the lifestyle of others than it would do to harm the few people who live in the places it would effect, but could these positives and negatives ever be adequately measured in order to form an undeniable argument? I doubt it.

They turn left.

FRANK: We're at the lifts again.

PROF: Yes, but these are different lifts.

FRANK: They look the same.

PROF: Don't all lifts look the same?

FRANK: Is that a philosophical question?

PROF: It's just up here.

They keep going.

PROF: It is possible that, in much the way we rationalise that a chicken killed for our consumption is acceptable because it provides nutrition, that we consider it acceptable to strip mine an untouched meadow to make resources for our use.

FRANK: But what does it all mean?

PROF: I suppose it means you shouldn't listen to anyone who tells you that mining up here is wrong – unless they're vegetarian.

FRANK: Well, that isn't a huge help to me, I'll be honest.

PROF: There are no finalities in morality. If there were we'd all be doing it. Ah, here we are. I told you I knew where it was. The stage door is that way. Good luck.

PROFESSOR disappears and FRANK steps aside.

Cut to:

Onstage. An ANNOUNCER stands behind a podium.

ANNOUNCER: Ladies and gentlemen, I have just received word that our next speaker has just arrived, and we're sorry for his lateness. He is, of course, the Foreign and Commonwealth Office Chief Scientific Advisor.

Just as FRANK goes to enter, a US MARINE appears in front of him.

PRIVATE: Can I see your identification please sir?

FRANK: My ID? Why?

PRIVATE: Sir, there are United States Diplomatic Personnel in there, I cannot let you in without a formal search and some kind of identification.

FRANK: I'm the FCO Special Scientific Advisor – I'm speaking next. I'm being announced right now.

PRIVATE: And do you always wear a bathrobe to speaking engagements sir?

FRANK: No, of course not.

PRIVATE: And would you care to tell me why you're wearing one now?

FRANK: It's a long story.

ANNOUNCER: He has recently been appointed to the post after the tragic case of snow-blindness contracted by the former Chief Scientific Advisor, who we wish a speedy recovery.

FRANK: You see, it is me. Please, it's already been a strange enough day without me having to prove who I am to a soldier

PRIVATE: For your information sir, I am a United States Marine. I'm going to have to search you sir.

FRANK: Fine.

The MARINE begins searching FRANK.

FRANK: The Marines? Why are you here?

PRIVATE: We have a base in the area sir.

FRANK: I'll bet everyone wants that posting.

PRIVATE: The military presence is increasing and will continue to increase, and if called upon any service man or woman will do their duty.

FRANK: Look, I'm wearing a bathrobe, would you just stand easy or what you say.

ANNOUNCER: I can see he's just arrived, and it looks like he's wearing… Oh my… He began his career as a researcher at the Burton Institute before moving to Applied Dynamics…

FRANK: Why is there so much military up here?

PRIVATE: In a word.

FRANK: Yes?

PRIVATE: Russia.

FRANK: Of course.

PRIVATE: Russia has thirteen airfields, ten air-defence
    radar stations, sixteen deep-water ports, ten search-
    and-rescue stations and six fully operational military
    bases in the Arctic, and a fleet that includes thirty-five
    submarines, six missile cruisers, and a nuclear missile
    cruiser. Who do you think is going to combat that sir?
    The Canadians.

FRANK: I suppose I hadn't really thought about it.

PRIVATE: Well, you're an advisor now sir, so you're
    going to have to start thinking about it. Okay, you're
    cleared for entry.

ANNOUNCER: Please help me welcome to the stage,
    Frank Montgomery.

FRANK: That's my cue.

PRIVATE: Good luck, sir.

FRANK makes his way to the stage.

FRANK: Thank you, for that introduction. You'll also
    have to forgive the bathrobe, I've had a somewhat
    unusual day and I didn't have time to change. I've
    spent most of the day meeting people with a big stake
    in this game, if you can call it a game, and trying to

form my own opinions – And the only conclusion I can come to is that…

ANNOUNCER: Ladies and gentlemen, it is now one o'clock, we will break for one hour for lunch. Please be back in an hour and a half.

FRANK stands onstage as everyone leaves.

FRANK: That's it? That's all the time I get.

ANNOUNCER: No, you had half an hour. You were late.

FRANK: Yes, I heard they take lunch seriously around here.

ANNOUNCER: For some, it's a matter of life and death. Nice robe, by the way.

FRANK leaves the stage.

Cut to:

The Hotel Jack London breakfast room, later that night. FRANK is sitting at the table with a whiskey on the rocks in his hand. He is watching the ice melt in his glass. After a few moments, the GIRL from that morning walks by.

GIRL: Hello.

FRANK: Hi. I am allowed to be in here, aren't I?

GIRL: Yes, of course.

FRANK: The door was open. I just came in.

GIRL: It's no problem. You looked like you were in a daydream.

FRANK: Oh, yes. I was just watching the ice melt.

GIRL: We do that a lot up here.

FRANK: I suppose you do.

Silence. She hands him a box of tea bags.

GIRL: I brought this for you.

FRANK: …Tea?

GIRL: Yes, I don't know if it's the type you'd like but I wanted you to have it.

FRANK: Thank you.

GIRL: You're welcome.

FRANK: Thank you very much.

GIRL: Oh, you also left this on the table.

She hands him his speech from earlier.

FRANK: Ah, my speech. Turns out I didn't need it anyway.

He looks over it.

GIRL: Are you okay? You seem a little less upbeat than you did this morning.

FRANK: …Yes, I'm fine. Thank you for asking.

GIRL: How was your day?

FRANK: It was… Strange.

GIRL: Oh, the Council meeting? How was it? If you can tell.

FRANK: It was interesting. Chaotic. A lot of people, a lot of plans, and a lot of intentions.

GIRL: All good, I hope.

FRANK: Sadly, not all. In fact, I think you're going to see quite a lot of transformation in this place over the next few years, and it won't all be for the best.

GIRL: Still, it will bring some good things?

FRANK: I really tend to doubt that it will. It's a shame. There is something about it up here.

He begins reading through his speech.

GIRL: A lot of people say that.

FRANK: There was a time, not that long ago, when this was a final frontier. A wilderness that inspired imaginations. Now we're talking about runway widths and tourism regulation. *(About his speech.)* That's a very good conclusion.

GIRL: To the speech? Can I hear it?

FRANK: Yes. I suppose it would be nice if someone got to. *(Reading.)* It isn't a question of want and not want, everyone wants the Arctic to remain untouched and perfect, but the question is what will they, and what we will, give up to secure it. Do we care enough to change our way of life, or do we not? As long as our collective goal is economic prosperity and growth, the Arctic will be exploited to the limits of its existence. If, and it's a big if, we can find a goal larger than short term economic gain, then it will be saved." It doesn't sound as good out loud as it sounds on paper.

GIRL: I thought it was nice.

FRANK: Well I was going for paradigm shifting, but nice is nice I suppose.

GIRL: I'd better get going anyway, I'm late for the turndown service.

FRANK: Right you are. Thank you for the tea. Oh, and can you do me a favour?

GIRL: Of course.

FRANK: Tomorrow morning, if you see me reaching for a yogurt, stop me.

The GIRL exits.

FRANK lifts up his drink. Again, he spends a few seconds watching the ice melt.

The End.

By the same author

An Incident at the Border
9781849434355

Bunnies
9781849434676

WWW.OBERONBOOKS.COM

Follow us on www.twitter.com/@oberonbooks
& www.facebook.com/OberonBooksLondon